THE HOUSE

The Truth of Who You Are Lives Within You

Melissa Crane, DC MS HHP

Ordering Information: Quantity sales. Special discounts are available on quantity purchases by corporations, associations, and others. For details, contact the publisher at the address above.

ISBN: 978-1-7330955-6-3
Nirvana Wellness Publishing

To the Wayshower, the Trailblazer, the Lightworker, the Starseed, the Rebellious Spirit, the Unseen, the Unheard, and the Misunderstood:

Keep shining.

&

To my family, with all my heart.

Table of Contents

"We all have storms and stories
inside our star made bodies
that even the night sky cannot hold.

This is why we are on this earth;
to learn how to love each other,
to learn how to love and hold ourselves."

-Nikita Gill, A Universal Truth, <u>Fierce Fairytales</u>

Introduction

Hi there. My name is Melissa Crane. I've been on a pretty crazy life journey, and I'm sure you have too, especially if you've been guided to read this book. It's been packed full of ups and downs, twists and turns. Spiritual awakening, ascension, self-discovery, and divine union within oneself, are all hefty processes that aren't for the faint of heart.

It can be overwhelming when Spirit comes into your life in a way that can't be ignored, forcing you to open your eyes and truly see yourself, *all of yourself.* I've learned some massive life lessons through Spirit, many times the hard way, sometimes more than once until I finally 'got it.' I'm still learning and growing, discovering new ways of being through curiosity and exploration, and I will do this for as long as I'm here in Earth School.

I've struggled to find my place in this world, never really knowing where I genuinely fit in, often feeling misunderstood, and a bit like a black sheep. For much of my life, I struggled with feeling unseen, unheard, and like I wasn't enough. I was scared to speak up and share my truth because I was afraid of being rejected. For a long time, I wasn't able to acknowledge my worth, yet I was hurt when others didn't see it.

There were many times when I thought it would be easier to just give up. For many years, I distracted myself from the mental and emotional turmoil through substance abuse, over-exercising, restricted eating, relationship hopping, and anything else that took my focus away from the depression I was feeling at the time.

I held deep wounds within my soul. Many times I wondered what all the pain, suffering and heartache were for. Nothing ever seemed to change, even after I thought I had 'done the work' required. It felt like I didn't matter, that is until I surrendered and allowed Spirit to guide me. I traveled deep into my shadowy depths and questioned everything I had previously accepted as truth. My perception began to change, and that's when my life began to change. The beliefs I held about myself shifted. Forgiveness and compassion for myself and others came to the forefront, and little by little, the light I held within grew brighter, and the love I had for myself became stronger and unconditional.

I needed to de-condition myself from ways of BE-ing throughout all my living years. I had to embrace my fear and to free myself from shame and judgement, both self-imposed and otherwise. I journeyed through a cycle that, to me, felt like death and rebirth. All I wanted and prayed for was to feel better and to be *me* again. The confusing part was that *I* didn't even know who *I* was anymore! I was having a complete identity crisis, or as some may say, an ego-death. Everything that I once knew to be "my life" no longer felt right, nor was what I wanted. I felt like a snake who had just shed its skin, vulnerable and sensitive. I felt like a butterfly who had just come out of its chrysalis, transformed and confused. I felt like a baby bird who was just pushed out of the nest and told to fly, frightened, yet free.

I had to practice having the courage to speak about all of this and to show up as the person I was beginning to remember I was, without wearing any masks. It was like coming out of a deep coma. Little by little, certain things would trigger memories of my soul's divine purpose, and of a life once lived in a world where magic was real, light was our language, and love was the way.

A world free of fear, shame, guilt and judgement, where we shared our unique gifts with one another and lived together in peace and harmony.

A world where we respected the Earth as our mother, where time didn't exist and we were guided by the planetary alignments.

A world where we allowed the seasons to move us

and feed us. In a world where we listened to our bodies and understood that they were an instrument used to experience the emotions of God, source intelligence. A world upon which we weaved a beautiful web with our light while co-creating and experiencing our own unique versions of Heaven.

Over time, I began to remember that I am a lightworker. I am a starseed. I am a wayshower. I am a spiritual leader. I am a powerful, divine, radiant being of light. I am a channel for grace and joy. I am here to help anchor in the New Earth. I walk alongside angels and galactic beings and I am continuously in a state of balance, flow, creation, death and rebirth. I am one with All That Is. I am that, I am.

As I write this, the world is in a global lockdown due to Covid-19, and the fear, panic, and uncertainty that has gripped the collective mind are palpable. Even before this crisis, humanity was already facing a pandemic, that of people-pleasing, guilt, sadness, shame, and fear.

Harvesting all this dense, low vibratory emotional gunk is what will kill you over time, or at the very least, will eventually result in an explosion of violence and rage for some.

There are infinite experiences to be had, yet the raw emotions they provoke are the common denominator. The feelings that lie beneath the surface, and the emotions that are triggered, are the magical ingredients for compassion. Whether it's gut wrenching sadness, deep shame, or agonizing fear; whether it's insurmountable grief, hot-blooded anger, or rage; or whether it's ecstatic bliss or unconditional love, these *feelings* are what people resonate with.

The word 'emotion', *originates from the Latin word 'emotere,'* literally meaning *energy in motion*. Emotions are to be felt as they arise, without judgment. They are meant to flow and to move energy through and out of your body. In my opinion, emotions are signals for us to pay attention. As they arise, allow them to speak to you. Allow them to show you where the energetic obstructions are in your body. Do not block or repress them, for they need to move. This is where two very different Eastern and Western health care philosophies overlap. The Chakra System, the Meridians, their associated emotions and elements, and their location in the human body, are all intricately connected and offer a map to how outside energies affect our internal world. We are the Maestros of a brilliant divine instrument.

The spiritual quest isn't one of glitter and rainbows, and frolicking with unicorns in a fairytale land, all the while turning your back to the corrupt world of injustice and control. It's quite the opposite. It requires you to walk directly into the storm and to discover everything you have been subconsciously enslaved to.

It will bring you face to face with your shadows. It requires commitment and courage to keep digging into the strata of your soul as you uncover your darkest fears, wounds, and deep-set patterns. It forces you to open your eyes and recognize how you were the only one keeping yourself stuck. It shows you how everything you claimed to be a victim of actually existed as an opportunity to reclaim your power and rise to glory. Ascension takes you on a humbling journey to ask for immense compassion and love for yourself. It asks you to forgive yourself for everything you have done that betrayed your heart.

The long and winding road to self, albeit rough and jagged, will help you witness the most exquisite beauty your eyes will ever be graced with.

The process of transformative alchemy cleans the lens through which you previously perceived your life, allowing you to see clearer and understand more than you ever have before. You begin to see your life in a new and ever-expanding way and things that held you back become propelling forces that move you forward. The love that you feel in, and for your body, dissolves any fears left standing in the way of your deepest desires. As fear dissolves, space opens up, which will allow for new opportunities to merge and come into union with everything you yearn for. All that you desire is no longer sought for outside of yourself, for once it is cultivated, found, and felt within, your desires will find you. Everything you desire is already within your heart, and as we all learn to live and be guided from that space, the place where our truest essence and divinity resides, we will be met with experiences in our outer world that will reflect that back to us.

Every moment, every breath, and every thought exists as an opportunity to choose your direction. With one step at a time, move along your new path, observe your surroundings with each new step, and take time to feel along the way. There is no rush, for there is no other moment than NOW.

I'm excited to share my story with you. Even though it's based upon my personal and unique picture show, I believe the underlying energies, the story itself, and the frequencies it holds, will connect with your heart and soul. If however, what I share doesn't resonate with you, then please do not accept it as *your* truth. We all walk through life using our own unique set of eyes and with our own unique antennas. As we ascend, expand our awareness and raise our consciousness, we must learn how to use discernment as we relate to everyone and everything outside of ourselves. Just because someone has a specific view on something doesn't make it the ultimate truth, especially if it doesn't sit well within you. That said, it doesn't make it untrue either. When feelings of dissonance arise, know that you are being offered an opportunity to explore them deeper, rather than simply jumping to judgement of the source from which they are delivered. All I ask is that you continue reading with an open mind and an open heart and feel what comes up for you. As with anything you hear or see or read out in the world, take what resonates, and leave the rest.

It's my hope that the teachings shared throughout this story will help you surrender to the guidance of your inner compass and trust its calibration to your true north. Let this journey purify you, warm your heart, and bring sweetness to the container of your soul. Allow yourself to awaken to your spiritual divinity.

As you read on, you may find yourself speculating about which parts of my story happened exactly as told, and which have been embellished by my imagination. It may shock you to know that it's all true. I believe the best experiences we have in life have been created in our hearts, with the help of our imaginations...

"By volunteering to go along on this ride, it has revealed to me who I am, what we are all a part of, and what I came here to do on this Earth. I am here to assist with the ascension of the planet and to help the collective consciousness shift from 3D to 5D by sharing my unique truth whilst embodying love and compassion. It is my highest hope, with the purest intention, from my heart to yours, that by sharing my story, it will lend guidance, support, solace, strength, courage, and light, during the dark and stormy times of life that we all inevitably go through."

— Melissa Crane, DC MS HHP

Part 1

The House

———◆———

Gather 'round, Dear One. Bring your blanket, grab a cup of cacao, and get comfortable. Settle into your space, then into yourself, and take a deep breath. Open your heart. I would like for you to put your imagination cap on as I lead you on a journey. We will be visiting a place you know, a place that lies deep within your heart. I invite you on this journey with me, to be Co-Captain of this ship, as we venture together, back home...

The Creation

Let us begin by creating the setting. I would like for you to envision your Dream Home. From the outside, what does the exterior of your house look like? What types of materials is it made of? What color is it? How big is it? What shape is it?

You can imagine anything at all, but you must imagine it first, in order to create it. What surrounds your home? What do you see? Is it sheltered in a large city? Is it in the middle of a country plain? Is it nestled within a quaint village, or secluded far back in the woods? Is your Dream Home near mountains, or a shimmering lake? Take a moment to picture where your Dream Home will be, and take in all of the details.

What sounds do you hear? Listen closely. Are there birds chirping, children laughing, or lawnmower engines humming? What do you smell? What aromas tantalize your nostrils in your dream landscape? Remember, this is your dream, your creation, your vision, and it's all about what makes you HAPPY!

I invite you to take a moment now to notice how you FEEL as you hold the image of your Dream Home in your mind. Imagine yourself walking around it, touching it, and seeing its intricacies. Take a deep breath in and bring life to your vision with every inhale. Fill yourself up with deep knowing in your heart, that this house is all yours, then exhale with gratitude as it's on its way to you now. Tap into all of your senses and 'just be' with your creation, truly as if you are there, right here and now.

Now, approach your front door and open it. Imagine yourself walking into your house. Look around. What do you see? What adorns the walls? What colors do you see? Are there multiple levels in your home? Are there multiple rooms? Explore every nook and cranny of your house. Take some time to get to know this unique and beautiful house of your dreams. Go ahead, I'll wait...

Now one thing I must tell you is that this house is *magical!* It has superpowers, secret levels, invisible hallways, and mysterious veils! This house can transform itself, and has the ability to fix, update and remodel itself, because... You hold the *Magic Wand*. Oh yes! You, My Dear, hold the most highly acclaimed, innovative technological advancement of all time, right in the palm of your hands.

The Invitation

Begin to imagine that you've been living in this house for some time now and every day you wake up feeling even more grateful than the last. You're so proud of what you've created, and rightfully so, as your house is a true gem. You utterly adore it, and living here fills you with joy and contentment.

One morning, as you rise from a peaceful night's sleep, you see something unusual – an envelope, lying within reach. It shimmers with glittery fairy dust and smells of sweet musk. There's a silver seal with a dab of purple wax, imprinted with an unusual geometric symbol. Perplexed, you peel back the wax and open the envelope. Ever so gently you pull out a beautifully handcrafted and meticulously pressed piece of paper. You rub the soft fibers between your fingers, then carefully unfold the paper. It's adorned with glistening gold trim and perfectly hand-scribed lettering. The message states:

"Congratulations! You have just won your dream vacation! You may choose

to go anywhere in the World you want, all expenses paid. All responsibilities and obligations have been cleared from your schedule. Pack your bags now because you're about to experience the best times of your life! You deserve this! You are extremely worthy of this trip and the time has come for you to receive it!

Your magic wand will take you there. Hold it in your hands and place it against your heart. Close your eyes and visualize yourself in the center of the geometric symbol that is imprinted on the purple wax seal. Once you see yourself in the center of the symbol, visualize where you want to go, and see yourself as already being there. Allow yourself to feel the elements of what surrounds you. How does it feel to be in your unique paradise? Feel it all, My Love. Take a deep breath and as you exhale, off you go! Enjoy the ride, Dear One! I love you."

You gasp and ask yourself, '*Is this for real? Where did this come from?*' Well, never mind that, for I'm here to tell you, yes it is for real, so get ready to have the experience of your lifetime! As the news begins to settle in, so too does your excitement. Your heart begins to race and you are covered in chills. You are in shock. How could so much goodness come into your life at once? First, your Dream Home, now your Dream Vacation. You feel so incredibly blessed and you are overcome with wonder and anticipation for what this epic vacation holds in store! Then you notice the fine print…

> *"P.S. You must find a family of three – a couple and their young child – to take care of your house while you are on vacation. No one else is allowed in your house, except this family. Picture who you want to take care of your house, and so it will be."*

You sit and begin to ponder about the type of family you would want to reside in your Dream Home while you are experiencing your Dream Vacation. After all, you really do *love* your house and you can't leave it in the hands of just anyone!

I invite you now to continue painting in the details, as I guide you through the dynamics of this ideal family, and the rest of this story…

The Family

One of the partners is super outgoing and incredibly strong, extroverted and magnanimous, full of energy and passion. This partner loves to be out in the world and is a force of compassionate power in service to others. They do this because it makes them feel purposeful and in alignment with who they truly are. They take inspired action, and they are resilient and diligent about serving their soul's mission. This in turn allows them to provide security, stability, and abundance to their beloved partner and child. We will call this person, *Yang*.

Now, let's imagine the other partner. This beautiful divine being, in its truest essence, is filled with joy and love just by BE-ing. They tend to their beloved partner and child, nurturing them with the gentlest love and care. This partner moves with graceful elegance and has a calm and peaceful presence. They are quiet and soft, yet hold great power. They understand the importance of taking things slow and they flow through life with ease. They enjoy rituals of self-care and treat themselves with beautiful clothing, delicious whole foods, and fragrant natural oils to nourish their skin. They are lovers of the night sky, the stars, and the moon. They have an innate gift to create comfort wherever they are. We will call this person, *Yin*.

Together, Yang and Yin form a perfectly balanced pair. These polar opposites are magnetized to one another, seeing themselves in each other's eyes, and feeling each other within their hearts. They honor and respect one another. They appreciate each other's uniqueness and celebrate their differences. They communicate in a loving way. They are honest and loyal and kind. They trust one another completely. They are true divine counterparts and their love for each other is pure and unconditional.

Let us imagine their child. This child is six years old and still very innocent. This child looks at everything with a sense of wonder and curiosity. The child's mind creates worlds of fantasy and magic. They are led and guided by their SOUL purpose, which is to have fun, to play, and to explore new things. They have no fear because they have no reason to be afraid. They aren't jaded or biased, and they hold no sense of shame, anger, or hate.

They intrinsically *know*, because of how they *feel*, that they are truly loved by their parents. They know and trust they are safe. They know they will never be betrayed or abandoned by their parents. They are heard, seen, appreciated, and celebrated for who they are. They are encouraged to DREAM BIG and to follow their dreams, to nurture them, and believe in them until their dreams become reality.

This child is confident that their parents will always offer loving support and guidance, whenever the child wants to experience something out in the world, something they are curious about and called to explore. They know too, that if an experience happens to make them feel defeated and sad, their parents will be there to comfort them, and to encourage them to hold their head up high. This child brings their parents so much joy, and this child, through their parents' example, learns and understands what true unconditional love *feels* like.

Together, this family lives in perfect harmony. They each provide for one another and the family as a whole, thereby creating balance, and a sense of equal give and take. Together they are complete, and they co-create their lives upon a solid foundation of peace and unity.

I would like for you to take a moment to sense how you're FEELING as you imagine this family residing in your Dream Home. Bring your awareness to your heart space. Do you feel a sense of calm or comfort? Do you feel as though you could trust them to take care of your house?

If so, I invite you to say, "Yes. I trust them. I am safe to enjoy my dream vacation, for I know my house is protected."

You pack your bags with only what you need, nothing more. Sitting on the floor, beside your bags, holding your magic wand in one hand and the envelope in the other, you open the letter again. The shape on the seal is a star, created with a series of triangles. As you study it closer, you realize it's a tetrahedron consisting of two interpenetrating three-sided pyramids, a Merkaba. You place the letter on the floor and raise the magic wand in your hand, then you bring it to rest next to your heart. You close your eyes and imagine yourself standing in the center of the Merkaba. Slowly the vision of your Dream Vacation begins to emerge.

You imagine the sights, sounds, and smells that surround you. Your skin tingles with a vivid sensation of everything around you as all your senses become engaged. You feel gratitude for this moment, and for the tools you have been gifted, to make your wildest dreams come true.

With your eyes closed and absolute focus, you take a deep breath in. You can't help but wonder, 'Is this even going to work?' and as you release your breath slowly, you open your eyes to find yourself exactly where you were. It didn't work! Frustrated, yet determined, you think to yourself that there must be more to this puzzle. What did you miss?

You look at the envelope on the floor, and your eyes are drawn to the purple wax. Could that be it you ask? Once again you close your eyes and focus inward with complete awareness, as you imagine yourself in the center of the Merkaba. Your paradise emerges, this time wrapped in a purple, translucent, sphere of light. You feel as if you have arrived. You take a deep breath in and fill your heart with gratitude, and as you exhale the word "Believe," loudly sounds in your ears, and suddenly off you go! As you open your eyes, you are struck with amazement as you realize you have arrived in Paradise.

The Veil

Let us now imagine that you are on your holiday and having the time of your life. You are experiencing things you never thought possible. After a joyous, carefree day of living purely in the moment, you decide to do a quick check-in of your house, just to see how things are going. Luckily, you have your *Magic Wand* which gives you the ability to teleport yourself back to your home sanctuary.

Out of respect for the family, you visit from behind a veil of invisibility, so they can go on with their day uninterrupted by your presence. Don't worry, as this arrangement was agreed upon before the family decided to stay at your house, and you are not invading their privacy.

They can also send a virtual call to you, in case they are having any trouble with the house, or if they want help. All they need to do is to call out your name and you'll hear them. Your *Magic Wand* will buzz to notify you, and you can teleport back there in an instant, to offer your guidance and support. Though you're still behind the veil, the family will be able to *sense* that you are there. They are so grateful for this top-of-the-line security system. They can call for your help at any time, and it comforts them and gives them faith and trust, to know they are safe, and you are only a moment away.

Now and then, you teleport back from paradise in your Merkaba and sit with them from behind the veil. As you sit with the family and exist within their energetic bubble of love, you bear witness to the relationships they have with one another. These relationships can only be described as pure perfection. You are humbled and in complete awe of the tight bonds the family members have with each other. You are so grateful they chose to leave wherever they came from to watch over your home.

Your relationship with this family grows and deepens. The love they have instilled within your home, and with one another, is so profound that it touches a place deep in the sacred core of your heart. It inspires you.

You begin to leave gifts and souvenirs for them as tokens of your appreciation. You take note of their likes and dislikes. You take note of the wishes and desires they speak of and long to have. You would do anything for them because you love them and want them to be happy, and you are grateful that they are staying and taking such good care of your house while you are away.

The Storm

One day, while gallivanting around in paradise, you hear a startling cry for help and your *Magic Wand* starts buzzing out of control. A terrible storm has shrouded your house in darkness. The skies have opened up and rain is pouring down, flooding the landscape. The wind howls and bends the trees near breaking. Thunder booms and powerful lightning creates an inferno, setting buildings on fire, burning them to ashes. The storm is so destructive the virtual lines of communication with the family become static and eventually are lost.

The family members are no longer able to sense your presence and become overwhelmed with fear. They cry out to you for help but they can't hear you or feel your answer. You try relentlessly to get through to them; you even try to come back from paradise and cut your vacation short, but no matter how hard you try you can't seem to get back! The virtual teleportation units must be down.

You do the only thing you can: use your Magic Wand to create a holographic screen, through which you can check in on them from afar. As the family comes into view, you stare at the screen, never taking them out of your sight. You wait patiently for an opportunity, in any way or form, that will allow you to be with the family once more.

The storm ceases to let up. The darkness lasts for days on end, then days turn into months, and months turn into years. The family unit, once full of hope, light, and joy, begins to collapse. The ties that bound them together, once so tight and strong, become weaker and begin to unravel. The tightly bound cords that connected their hearts begin to dissolve into mere threads.

Yang, that courageous, mighty, and ambitious partner, continues to go out into the storm, remaining ever so determined to fight through it to support their beloved Yin and child. Meanwhile, the peaceful, quiet Yin helplessly tries to restore the comfort that once existed in the house but struggles to keep up. After a while, both Yang and Yin become exhausted and worn out. They lose their ability to communicate, and swallow and choke on their words to each other. Sadly, they begin to lose faith and trust in each other, as well as in themselves. Though each feels they are doing their best, playing their part, and fulfilling their role, the storm is too powerful and has begun to get the best of them.

After a long day of exerting their passionate inner force, the ambitious Yang comes home tired and irritated, feeling as though all of their hard work was for nothing. No longer does Yang greet their family upon coming home, nor do they receive nurture with a loving embrace, much less warmth or compassion. Yang fears they are letting the family down and begins to harvest immense amounts of shame and guilt. Yang feels like a complete failure, sad and unworthy of forgiveness.

Yin becomes depleted and despondent and is no longer able to partake in daily self-care rituals. There is no longer time to do any of the things they love, things that once filled their cup with joy overfloweth, and allowed them to give to others from a place of abundance.

As a result of Yin's tireless giving, the cup has become dry, yet Yin continues to pour from it with every ounce of energy left. This leads Yin to feel the same as Yang. Both partners begin cultivating self-deprecating thoughts, and beliefs of guilt, shame, unworthiness, and fear. They are very sad and need help, yet they fail to recognize that the help they desperately seek would be found in each other, by way of compassionate acknowledgment. If they could allow themselves to see their reflection in the other, and offer to the other what they need: compassion, love, and understanding, then a harmonious and balanced state of being would be restored once more. If they could once again see how by extending the same love which they share for their child, toward one another, they would be able to heal the pain they each feel so deeply within.

The storm prevails, however. It intensifies, becoming even more destructive, and not only does it cloud this awareness, but it also distracts the family from reuniting their hearts, and gaining the strength they need to overcome the storm. The threads that connect their hearts unravel and eventually sever. A gaping hole now exists between them, sucking away their power, and any last remaining hope to remedy their pain. The storm continues to cultivate the couple's emotional despair, eventually leading to anger and resentment. It's difficult for them to accept what life has become and they begin placing blame on each other for not doing more to prevent this travesty from occurring.

Meanwhile, their young child has hidden in its room so as not to witness its parents' angry outbursts. Frightened, and unable to understand what is happening, the child throws tantrums, but the parents are too distracted by the storm and their grief to notice their little one's plea for help.

Though the parents' main focus is to keep their child safe and protected at all costs, the storm has distracted them. They have forgotten how impressionable their young child is, and how the storm has been affecting the child. They have forgotten the naivete of children, and how the child is unaware of the many burdens the parents bear.

The child begins to act out in fear because its safety feels threatened. The bubble of love and peace in which the family existed before the storm has popped, leaving the child bare and vulnerable to the lingering heavy and emotional energetic debris. The child has become fully immersed in the tension that exists within the house. The child observes how hard the parents work, and how tired, angry, and sad the parents have become; and it upsets the child. The child hates seeing its parents so unhappy and feels as though the parents no longer love each other.

Although the child is safe and loved, it is becoming more doubtful with each passing day, questioning everything it once believed to be true. The unconditional love the child once felt and knew to exist has become a distant memory. The peace, harmony, and togetherness the family once experienced has been replaced with separation and conflict. The child wonders if it has done something wrong and worries it is to blame for the parents' distress. The child wonders if the parents wouldn't be so upset if they didn't have to work so hard or worry so much about keeping them all happy and safe.

It seems however, that the storm is here to stay. It's difficult for the child to accept because the child doesn't like feeling this way, nor does it like how the parents argue. The child feels helpless, as though it has no control and no say. The child knows that life doesn't have to be this way and can't understand why their parents are letting the storm win.

The child becomes defiant and makes any attempt to revolt against the storm. The storm however, is far too strong, and to its dismay the child learns that this is far too great a task to take on alone. The child hides and cries, and wishes for everything to go back to the way it was before the storm, when all was well. The child feels helpless and alone, and retreats to its hiding spot where it prays for help or some kind of miracle that will save the day.

The child decides that if it's ever able to get out and escape from this wretched storm, it will do whatever it takes to avoid ever being in another one. The child imagines that if the family does indeed escape the storm, they will create their very own Heaven on Earth, where the Sun will always rise and dry up the rain. The child dreams of creating a world where joy abounds, where peace and harmony are restored, and where the family will be bound together in love once again.

After many hours, the child begins to devise a plan. It observes everything, taking note of what feels good and what doesn't. Within the child's little body and mind, 'seeds' of what the child likes begin to collect, and the child holds tightly onto these 'feel good' memories and experiences. The child envisions these seeds growing into more experiences that feel good, and eventually, this will give way to a whole new world for the child that feels good. The child holds and protects the 'seeds' and keeps them close to its heart.

At the same time, the child keeps note of everything that doesn't feel good and reminds itself to keep those bad seeds out. Every time the child experiences something that causes a yucky feeling, the child collects the bad seed in a locked box. The box is kept hidden, deep down within, as the child wants to make sure that it never makes the mistake of accidentally planting a 'bad seed'.

What the child fails to understand is that by doing so, they now carry ALL potentiality within, through all the memories, beliefs, and experiences that are locked up and hidden inside. The child is holding onto the memories, the experiences, and the beliefs that feel good, that which the child wants to create more of, AND all the negative memories, beliefs, and experiences that feel bad, that which the child doesn't want to create more of.

As the family begins to create their new world according to the child's desire, by planting the good seeds of positivity and hope, they unknowingly plant the bad seeds alongside, for they are one in the same. *The child is the seed, you see...*

They intend to create a world of unconditional love, however, since everything 'bad' has been locked away, it is blocking the 'good' from fully rooting. The child doesn't know that to grow your own Heaven on the Earth, the good must be able to wrap its arms around the bad, through *forgiveness.*

We must be grateful for what the bad memories, experiences, beliefs, and feelings have taught us. This is the most important key for creation: *integration,* and it is in the child's hands. All the child must do is unlock the box containing the bad seeds to fully integrate them, without separating the good from the bad, as all of it came from love. If the child can see everything it has experienced and collected from life experiences, from its parents, and from living through the storm, as opportunities to choose what it wants, then the child can create and live in their Heaven on Earth. Unfortunately, the child doesn't understand this critical concept, and to its detriment, its plan to live in Heaven on Earth will forever be ravaged by the storm.

All this time you have watched from afar on your virtual screen, and your heart breaks as you watch while this family falls apart, and your house crumbles. If they could only see what you see, they would realize they have what it takes to save themselves.

You've seen Yin and Yang enter into a deep depression and turn to anything that distracts them from their pain and suffer. You've watched as their child grows older and becomes filled with rage and hatred for the storm that has torn the family apart. You've watched as they search desperately for answers and cling to anything that helps fill the void in their hearts. The family's pure sweetness and joy for life have been lost.

Decades go by and eventually the storm passes, by then so much damage has been done, the family has all but given up. They feel as if it's a lost cause to even try to rebuild, much less even know what to do, or where to begin. The child's plans to create a new world have been tossed aside, even though they still hold the key to save them all. The family is filled with shame and guilt for not being able to maintain your beautiful home as they had promised. They are embarrassed and afraid of the judgment you will bestow upon them when you return, if indeed you ever do.

You heard their cries as they begged each night for your help and saving grace, but since you couldn't get through to them, they lost all hope and faith in you. You never once stopped loving them, but they could no longer *feel* that love. Even when you were able to send them gifts and tokens, as little signs to let them know you were still there, they failed to recognize them. They were lost in the shuffle of day-to-day life. They felt trapped, as their thoughts and emotions held them hostage, leaving no way to escape from this dreadful prison.

One night, perhaps the darkest of nights, you witness each family member drowning in their sorrow and despair, numbed out by their distraction of choice in an attempt to escape the sadness and truth, as they'd come to know it. And finally, you watch as they pack their bags, with tears in their eyes, preparing to leave and make the journey back to where they came from.

The Awakening

So much emotion has been stirred up within you, and you begin to tremble and shake. You grip your Magic Wand with every ounce of being, frightened that if you can't get through to the family, if they can't hear or feel you, it might be the last time you ever see them.

"*NO!*" You scream as you fall to the floor. "*Please, don't go! I'm right here! I see you!*" You sob, kneeling over in despair. You feel their pain in every cell of your body. You feel the pain of abandonment, of betrayal, of shame, fear, and remorse. With your wand gripped tightly in your hand, you cry out between sobs and gulps of air, as if these are the final words you will ever say to them.

"*I forgive you for not being able to maintain my house. It's okay, it's not your fault. The storm was strong and you did the best you could. I saw how hard you tried. I'm sorry. I'm so sorry I couldn't be there beside you. I'm sorry you felt as if I didn't care. Please forgive me. I'm so grateful for all of you. I'm so grateful for you coming to reside in my house.*

I'm truly grateful to have witnessed a love so beautiful and true. Thank you for allowing me to see such sweetness and for allowing me to be a part of all of your lives. Thank you for changing my life. I have become a better person and I've learned so much from all of you! I love you. I love you. I love you."

You cry uncontrollably, rocking back and forth. With your head down and your eyes closed tightly, you try to console yourself. With both hands you bring the wand close to your heart, and suddenly a warm purple mist completely envelopes you. The wand begins to glow! Surprised, you jump to your feet and wipe the tears from your eyes as you shift your focus to the glowing wand.

Brighter and brighter it gets, as the colors fade into one another, first red, then orange, then yellow, green, blue, indigo, and finally violet. The end of the wand begins to flicker, and sparks explode outward. The wand becomes so hot you can't hold it any longer, and you watch helplessly as your fingers let go and the wand hits the floor, bursting into flames. The energy is intense and waves of heat surge through your body. As you lurch back from the exploding inferno, a massive, bird-like creature bursts forth from the flames.

There is so much light and heat radiating from the bird that you instinctively lift your arm and turn away. Through squinted eyes, you look back at the creature.

Its wingspan is immense, it's magnificent, breathtaking. You are not afraid. The bird's feathers are painted with the deep shades of a crimson red rose. As the feathers settle into place, tiny flecks of gold sparkle and shimmer in long, thin lines, down the length of its velvety wings. You try to look away but you're mesmerized.

You lock eyes with the creature, and immediately you understand it's here to help. You know that you are connected as partners. There are no questions. The majestic bird waits as you jump up and hoist yourself onto its back. Its massive wings spread out and slowly at first, then quickly, they beat the air, and the creature lifts itself and you, effortlessly up off the ground.

You grip the bird tightly as you soar up into the sky, flying through time and space. You fly through the stars and over rainbows, across dimensions, and through other galaxies. Then when you've gone a fair distance, you look back over your shoulder and see the magnificent planet Earth.

The bird turns and descends toward Earth. "*Look*", the bird says to you telepathically, "*that's where we go in.*" You see what looks like a metal portal that has been placed over the planet. You hold on tight as the creature flies faster and faster, directly toward a pinhole opening in the portal. You close your eyes and hold your breath, bracing yourself for impact.

As you enter the portal everything slows down as if time is suspended. You suddenly become aware of your surroundings. You open your eyes and you can see the beautiful Earth. You fly through the layers of Earth's atmosphere, entering in and coming closer to the planet. You fly over vivid, crystal blue oceans, and luscious, deep green rainforests. You soar across dry sandy deserts and seas of grassy plains, that seem to go on and on forever. You see pandas happily rolling and playing. There are herds of giraffes grazing over the Savanna, and wild mustangs galloping through fields of wildflowers. Huge glorious eagles soar closer and closer, then they fly alongside, guiding your way through the immense sky.

It's intensely liberating to witness such beauty from this perspective, everything is in perfect order and you feel peace all around. The wind is your shepherd as you soar through the sky on the back of the majestic winged creature. You look down and blink in disbelief, as you fly over your house. How worn and dilapidated it is. You can sense how exhausted the house is, from having endured the dark storm. Suddenly you notice Yin, Yang, and the child, standing with their belongings clutched in their arms. Your heart glows with love and joy when you see them. Here they stand, right here, right now, before your very eyes!

Down below, as the hopeless family prepares for their departure, they catch sight of a glowing fireball heading directly toward the house. They don't know what it is and panic sets in as they feel immense heat radiating toward them! It becomes hotter and hotter as the fireball gets closer! They seem paralyzed with fear and unable to move, as they grip one another tightly, not knowing what else to do. Everything is happening so fast! Yin and Yang embrace each other, with their child held tightly between them. Yin looks into Yang's eyes and they prepare themselves for the end.

The bird, with you still on its back, nosedives directly toward the house. It swoops down and envelopes the entire family.

In an instant: All Is One with All That Is. There is no you, no bird, no house, no family. There is only pure white light accompanied by an angelic symphony of sound. There is nothing, yet everything. There is no beginning and no end. There is only pure, ecstatic bliss, a feeling that no words are able to describe. It's as if everything is suspended in complete peace and stillness.

The Rebirth

You open your eyes and find yourself standing in the center of your house. It's quiet and serene, and as grand and impeccable as when you created it. You walk around your house, looking at the walls and what you adorned them with. Memories of the person you were, when you first placed them there, come flooding back. It feels like another lifetime, so much has happened since.

You are grateful to be back home. A sense of joy rises inside and you are filled with a sense of wonder and excitement. You walk through each room, seeing them for the first time with a new set of eyes. Suddenly, you feel a need to sink your feet into Mother Earth. Outside, you feel your feet on the ground beneath you and gaze up into the sky. You can feel the sun's warmth on your face as if you are being sweetly kissed by its rays. What just happened, you wonder. Was it real? Was it a dream? Just as quickly as thoughts about the family enter your mind, you hear their voices as a cosmic whisper from within.

"We are here, Sweet One. You will never be alone. We are you as you are us. We live within you and within this house. We are your mother. We are your father. We are your inner child. You are a radiant spark of stardust from the Divine. You are all-knowing. You are infinite consciousness, dressed up in your unique human suit and living in your unique world of existence. You have the power to create whatever you'd like. Magic is real and it's in your fingertips. The storm of darkness was just part of the mission to bring us all back together and to help you remember who you truly are."

You place your hands over your heart and can feel their presence within every cell of your body. Tears of heavenly grace run down your cheeks. You gasp quickly and then let out a long sigh. You take another deep, intentional breath in, and with your exhale, you allow your body to relax. You inhale again, this time breathing in gratitude for being alive, for feeling renewed, for feeling powerful and free. You exhale your breath of peace, hope, and love to all. You turn around, and as you begin to walk back towards your house, without any expectation of what's to happen next, you hear the family again as they whisper Ho'Oponopono, the traditional Hawaiian message of reconciliation and forgiveness:

"I'm sorry. Please forgive me. Thank you. I love you."

And you live happily ever after, in the infinite cycle of life and time.

Part II

Going Within

—⟨•⟩—

Shall we go inside? Come with me, take my hand. The family eagerly awaits your arrival...

As you enter their home, the family stands before you, greeting you with smiling faces and open hearts. They delightfully show you the way to the spacious family room. It's furnished with a large L-shaped couch, an oversized chair and ottoman, and strategically placed end tables. A beautiful stone fireplace with an incredible dark oak wood mantle adorns the room.

Emerald green houseplants grow happily upon bookshelves, in corners, and on tables within their beautifully hand-crafted pottery vessels of the Earth's clay. A fresh, airy breeze flows through the open windows, and bright, warm sunbeams splinter through the room.

The family invites you to have a seat. You gratefully move toward the large comfortable looking chair and sit. Your tired body melts into the chair and you feel yourself begin to relax. You didn't realize how much tension you were holding onto until you feel it begin to lift away. The family's loving presence surrounds you and provides a sense of safety and peace. You become aware of your belly, as it rises and falls with every breath.

The endless chatter and constant noise from everyday worries, anxieties, and endless pressures of To-Do's quiet down, and then effortlessly dissolve from your consciousness. Within the quiet stillness, your eyelids become heavy and you give in and allow yourself to rest. The sound of your breath guides you into a deep, restorative sleep.

The Child

After a long and peaceful sleep, you open your eyes to see the child standing near, watching you. The child's eyes are wide and gleaming brightly, as its joyful innocence and childlike spirit shine through.

The child is excited and eager to speak. You are curious and listen attentively to what the child has to say. *Do you want to see my room? Come on! Come with me!* The child says excitedly while grabbing your hand. The child enthusiastically pulls you up from the chair and leads you along a hallway and up a set of stairs. There's a door straight ahead, with a hand-written sign taped to the center. In big, crayon-scribed letters, it reads:

NO MONSTERS ALLOWED!

The door swings open as you both enter the room. The family's artwork covers the walls. They've made pictures of dragons, butterflies, and birds, with rainbows, smiling sunshine faces, and shooting stars. A large wooden chest, filled to the brim with toys and games, sits against the far wall. In a corner, you see a small table with colorful art supplies scattered over its top. A cute little rocking chair, fit for a small body sits in the corner, with a few stuffed animals and books lying around it on the floor. A play fort stands in the center of the room, made from strategically hung bed sheets and blankets. The child instructs you to get on your hands and knees and follow them inside.

The interior of their self-made sanctuary has been decorated with twinkling fairy lights, strung all around the ceiling. A battery-powered lantern lights up the fort, and stuffed animals and toy figurines line its perimeter. A bright pile of pillows fills the center of the fort. The child asks, *"Come and sit 'criss-cross applesauce' with me."* The child crawls onto your lap and settles into your arms, resting their back against your chest. You can feel the child's heartbeat as it begins to sync with your own. The child speaks:

"Do you remember what you used to dream about when you were little? Do you remember the games you used to play? Do you still remember how to use your imagination, and play make-believe? I love to play make-believe. It's my favorite game because I can be anything at all!"

You ponder the child's words for a moment as they have struck a chord of remembrance within your psyche. Those words... Make-believe. *Make... Believe...*

The child continues. *"Do you remember? You just have to imagine the kind of world you want to live in. It can be anything you want, anything at all! You can create a world where animals can talk, magic is real, and you are free to play all day. The only rule is that you must believe. When you believe, you become, and it's as simple as that! Sometimes I like to imagine that I have superpowers, and that I'm able to fly, and that I can make magical healing potions! Do you want to see my box of treasures?"*

The child reaches for a small wooden trinket box, etched with intricate designs. They open the box and reveal their most prized possessions, one by one. *"These are my magic crystals. This one helps me to feel happy when I'm sad. This one helps me to think of new ideas. This one helps me to focus when I'm making something. This one makes me feel super strong. This one helps me sleep better, and this one, hmmm...I'm not sure what this one is for, but it's pretty, and I just like it, a lot!"*

You silently giggle to yourself. The child's energy and excitement over showing and telling you about their special possessions, flutters like a hummingbird from flower to flower. The child places each one of the beautiful raw cut gems in your hand and tells you to hold them against your heart so you can feel their magical powers. They watch intently to make sure you are doing it correctly and once satisfied, they continue to pull from the box of trinkets. *"This is a golden key that will open anything that is locked. This is my hawk feather. This is my owl feather. This is my silver coin. This is my magic spray; it smells yummy and it keeps the monsters away. And this… is my magic wand,"* finishes the child.

The child places a small stick, wrapped with rainbow-colored ribbons, into your hands. *"I found it outside by my treehouse! The tree told me that it will give me extra power and will help make things come to life. I bet you could find one too! Maybe you could ask the tree to give you one?"* The child asks.

The child waves the magic wand around in the air as if orchestrating a great symphony for an invisible audience of fairy friends. Then the child cues the music to stop, and carefully puts the magic wand back into the box for safekeeping, along with the other sacred objects. Still snug in your lap, they reach over to your other side and pick up a leather-bound book. With a hushed voice, the child says, *"This is my secret journal. It's where I write about how I feel, and things I want to remember, and it's where I write down all of my wishes. Nobody is allowed to read it except me."*

Without opening it, they place it back down and rest their hand on top of its cover, pausing for a moment in reverence to its precious contents. The child looks around to see if there's anything else to show you, but that appears to be it. They crawl off your lap, take your hand, and lead you out of their fort, back downstairs to the family room. Yin and Yang are there, patiently waiting and smiling, as the child skips back into their loving arms.

Yin: the Mother

Yin rises from her seat and approaches you. Her silky red kimono flows behind, and her long hair cascades over her delicate shoulders, framing her oval face and youthful, dewy skin. Her gaze is soft, yet mysterious. Her eyes are as deep as the dark ocean, her beauty is breathtaking.

She extends her long slender hand, and when you take it, Yin leads you down a corridor. You approach a door on your left. Yin stops and motions for you to enter. You walk into a beautiful washroom, made with marble and hand-cut tiles, each carefully sealed with gold. Cascading plants, in all shades of green, hang in macrame nests, suspended from the wooden beams above. A gentle hum fills your ears and soothes your soul.

You see a large oval basin, fit for a queen, filled with crystal blue water. On the basin's ledge sit a variety of colorful candles, and glass containers filled with salts, fragrant oils, and delicate flower petals.

Yin lights the candles, one by one, as if she were bringing each one to life with the spark of her flame. It's hypnotic, watching her as she moves with graceful intent. She opens each container, greeting the pure essence with a long inhale, closing her eyes and allowing the aromatic signatures to tantalize her senses. She adds a little of each to the tub, in precise amounts, for a sacred healing soak. First, a scoop of Himalayan Sea Salts, then a few drops of Frankincense and Myrrh, and lastly, she sprinkles petals of Rose, Lavender, and Peony, delicately on top.

Yin turns and invites you to immerse yourself in the basin of water. You feel honored as you have never had such a luxurious bath drawn for you. You disrobe, step into the tub and slowly sink your body into the warm, sacred water. You let your head and upper body lean back and discover that you can effortlessly float, as the healing water holds and supports you.

Yin sits on a bench next to the tub and continues with your bath ritual by washing your hair. She is careful to keep the soap from getting into your eyes, while she lathers the shampoo, and gently massages your scalp. She reaches for a bronze pitcher, filled with clean, cool water, and rinses the suds from your hair. Yin speaks...

"My Dear Sweet One, how precious you are. I have drawn this bath for you as a reflection, and as a way for you to experience the divine grace of the sacred feminine, and the eternal love of the Divine Mother. Allow the water

to soothe you. *Allow the water to hold you, feel your body float. It is safe, I am here. How does it feel, Sweet One? How does it feel to float and be held? Surrender to the water and allow yourself to let go. Allow yourself to just be, it seems so simple, yet is quite possibly one of the hardest things to do. It all comes down to trust. Do you trust the water? Do you trust you will be supported if you relinquish all control? Are you able to trust in a force outside of yourself? Witness yourself as you are doing it right now, you see? Right here in this tub. Notice how you are held, how you float, and how all is well.*

Feel how the weight of your body seems to have disappeared; almost as if you and the water have become one. Allow your ears to dip beneath its surface, listen to your breath, and notice how your inhales and exhales sound like the ocean's tide. In and out, coming and going...

Surrender into the water and allow it to hold you, just as you were once held within your mother's womb. The mother's womb exists as a portal between worlds; the 'in between' of what was and what is to come. Within the womb, a baby is nourished and protected. The baby does not think of how it will be fed; it just is. The baby does not think of what it needs to grow, it just does grow, safely floating in the nourishing fluid of its mother's womb.

When was the last time you allowed yourself to feel such support and ease of mind? When was the last time you allowed yourself to trust in the Divine Sacred Mother, the Cosmic Mother of all that is, and allowed yourself to just be? When was the last time you listened to silence itself?

It is in the silence of nothingness where you are gifted the opportunity to experience all that is. When you have become quiet enough to hear only the sound of your breath and your heartbeat, you are gifted the opportunity to hear the purest essence of yourself. As you learn how to be with yourself, amidst the noise of all that surrounds you, you gain the ability to cultivate peace. By allowing your mind to rest, you gain the opportunity to access divine insight. When your heart and mind align, you become able to enter into a state of complete knowingness that all is well. You know you are safe and nourished, simply by BE-ing in the here and now, within the dark stillness of the sacred mother's womb.

A mother's love for her child is infinite. The child is and always will be a part of her, long after the time of birth. A mother's love is protective, as it will allow for nothing to harm the life she has created. A mother's love is fierce and she will stop at nothing to see that her child receives the best of what life can offer. When it comes to the love of her child, all else fails in comparison. A mother will do everything in her power to give her child a fulfilling life, a life of happiness, love, prosperity, health, and abundance in all forms. This is the Divine Mother's wish, to give *unto her child all she considers most high, and to offer her guidance through what she knows to be true, and always out of love.*

May I ask what it is that you hold most dear? What ingenious seed have you nurtured within yourself? What have you birthed into existence that is utterly invaluable? What do you hold within your ethereal womb that has yet to be birthed? Have you allowed yourself to let go of your creation? Can you allow yourself to be at peace, knowing that you've done all that you can and it's time to trust that all is well, and will be if you let go? Do you trust that your creation is worthy of being birthed and that it is safe to enter into the world outside of your protective womb? Are you able to trust in yourself, and your creation, and the ever-expansive and loving Universe of Mother-Father God-Source intelligence, though it's unseen by your human eyes? Do you have faith, Sweet One?

These questions allow for a glimpse into a mere fractal of the divine feminine's intricate and infinite web. Are you able to view yourself as a mother of creation, of life, and love? Are you aware that you carry seeds of divinity within yourself, inside of your protective womb?

Your gender makes no difference, as we all are creators, nurturers, and givers of life. Have you allowed the seeds which you have nurtured and nourished, to continue to grow outside of you, allowing them to see the light of day and to experience infinite bounty and bliss?

Do you value and honor this 'seed' so much that it excites you to share it with the world, allowing the magic of what you have cultivated within to be seen and shared for the betterment of all? Do you understand that for your creation to grow and expand in its divinity, you must let it go? For it will truly only be brought to life, once and if, it is released. You can only hold it within for so long before it loses the opportunity to live. There is a divine timing for everything, Dear One, and we must allow ourselves to abide by the greater forces that lie beyond our control.

The struggle and internal conflict of the mother illustrate childbirth itself. The pains of labor, the struggle of holding onto, and then letting go of love, and allowing your creation to be birthed into a world of uncertainty. Your creation now lives outside of you, exposed and vulnerable, and you must trust that it will be safe.

However, it is by living with what you have birthed when you are given the ultimate gift: the opportunity to experience joy and love of your self, in the form of another. Your creation offers its sacred reflection of your soul, thereby allowing you to see your divine potential. All of your love, all of your wisdom, all of what you are, birthed into existence, having a journey of its own, through the experience of becoming, and the doing and undoing of all that is meant to be.

Release fears around the 'what if', as those are not meant to be carried within. What we hold and carry within, also lives as our perception and reality. This is why it's so important to carry and hold onto only what you want to give life to, as that's how powerful you are!

See your worries, doubts, and fears for what they are. They have come from within you and ultimately from the power of unconditional love. Extend gratitude to those feelings as their purpose is to show you the true value and worth of your creation, and then, allow their energetic grip to dissolve, transmuting them into a fortifying strength.

Look at all the thoughts that arise and prevent you from birthing your creation and trusting in its ability to thrive. Fear, doubt, and worry are to be seen and acknowledged as they too have been given life by you, yet they have been pushed down below the surface, into the dark, and forced to exist as shadows. They are part of you, just as much as your light is part of you. Their existence is seeded from beliefs you've held and given life to, albeit in the depths of your soul.

When and if the shadows arise to be seen and to be heard, do not hush or hide from them, Sweet One. Instead, be the mother that you are to them, and offer your unconditional love unto them, as they too are your creations. Allow them to speak to you, for by taking their voice away, you will only cause them to carry shame. Love your worries, doubts, and fears as they are little children, and don't know the difference between 'right' and 'wrong', or 'good' and 'bad'. They don't know they live as shadows.

It's not their fault they were left to live in the dark. They are what they are, as they know no other way to be.

Begin to look at every shadow you hold within as part of yourself. Thank your shadows as they arise because they live to keep your creation safe. Perhaps your creation is what they have nestled next to, and they have grown to love it, and just don't want it to leave. Offer an apology to them for not honoring that which they are. Convey that it was not your plan to abandon them in the dark. See that their intention is pure, and extend your love unto them as they are a part of you. Love them with all your heart, and allow them to feel peace. They too want to feel loved and safe to exist just as they are. Extend your light to them, and help them see that which they cannot. Be the light within your shadows. Know your value, see your potential, trust your love, reclaim your power, and see yourself as the radiant spark of the divine that you are. You are the giver of life to both the light and the dark. You hold infinite power and potential for life itself within your heart. Honor the divine feminine and sacred mother within yourself. Remember who you are."

You open your eyes, still floating in the warm bath, wondering how long you've been floating there. Yin's message was profound. You feel as if you've just been in an altered state of mind and you were granted access to a place containing wisdom that until this moment has been locked and hidden from your view. Yin's words struck a chord, awakening something dormant within you. While lying in the water, Yin guided you to a place that needed to be seen and acknowledged. Never before have you conceptualized 'mothering' in this way, much less considered that your shadows would bring an entirely new level of compassion into your heart.

Yin retrieves a towel from the cabinet, unfolding and wrapping it around your body as you climb out from the tub. It's soft and warm. She gently presses it against your skin to dry you off. She motions for you to sit on the bench and she begins to comb through your hair gently. She pulls a bottle from her vanity, then pours out a golden oil into her hands, and warms it between her palms before anointing your skin. She rubs it over your shoulders and down your arms and back, leaving you feeling refreshed, cleansed, and renewed. Yin steps outside the room and waits as you get dressed. Together you walk back to the family room.

Yang: the Father

Yang welcomes his beloved Yin back into his arms. He kisses her forehead gently and does the same to his little one before he gets up. He approaches you and asks if you would now join him outside. He has a special glow about him and embodies a calm and gentle strength. You notice his naturally masculine frame. His skin appears thick, yet still allows for the subtle definition of his muscles to show through. His hands are calloused and rough, suggesting many hours of manual labor throughout his lifetime.

You follow Yang down a hallway that leads to a set of sliding glass doors. A golden light emanates from behind the doors, casting your shadow onto the floor beneath you. As you walk closer to the doorway, you and your shadow merge into one.

Yang opens the door and stands back for you to enter, then he follows you onto a large wooden deck. You stand together, overlooking hundreds of acres of fertile land, basking in the light of the setting sun; it's the Golden Hour, and it's divine. In this exquisite light, the breathtaking beauty brings tears to your eyes. You savor each moment, allowing yourself to truly feel what you see, syncing your eyes with your heart, as you bear witness to God.

You see boundless trees, a coy fish pond, a pathway of stone steps leading to a thriving garden of flowers, herbs, fruits, and vegetables, such abundance reflecting the love lying within the house it surrounds. You notice a bird feeder hanging next to a cute little nook, with a small table and chairs. Off to the side are a swing set and a sandbox. A wrought iron fence surrounds the area, offering just enough protection without hindering your view of the vast beauty lying beyond. Yang speaks:

"Isn't it beautiful? I created all of this, you know. Yin loves gardens; she loves smelling flowers. The pink roses are her favorite, she says they smell the sweetest. We grow all sorts of berries and vegetables, herbs too. Yin makes us the most delicious meals. She makes tinctures and teas, and healing salves of all kinds. She says Mother Earth holds the medicines. Yes, indeed; she's very wise."

Yang's voice trails off. The love he has for his partner is profound. He shifts his gaze from the garden back to where you are standing.

"This deck and patio, I laid it all out by hand. What a task that was. I didn't always know what I was doing, but help wasn't ever too hard to find. I built the swing set

too. Our little one loves to swing and make forts up there on the loft over the slide. It's their little clubhouse. I love to watch our child play. It's so inspiring, to see how children devour life, always learning, growing, and exploring, unafraid to try new things. They surely do keep me on my toes! I built the treehouse out front too! It was after a terrible storm hit. The poor tree lost so many branches, but afterward, it became the perfect base upon which to build something new.

I do it all for my family. It's important to take care of who you love, to provide for them, and make sure they're safe and secure. I'm happy to do it, and nothing brings me greater joy! It's my sole purpose... my SOUL's purpose. It fills me with a great sense of pride to see them enjoy everything I've built for them."

You can feel Yang's pride as he speaks, but it's not at all boastful or arrogant. He speaks from his heart. He shares his truth, without seeking validation and with nothing to prove.

"It's all about balance. Work. Play. Rest. It's about enjoying the moment and seeing the beauty and abundance that surrounds you. Take nothing for granted, as it can change in an instant. It's important to pay attention. You must be aware of your surroundings and yourself, keep your senses keen. The physical body is magnificent in this way. Its ability to sense, feel and perceive is incredible,

which is why it's so important to take care of yourself. Eat well, sleep well, stay hydrated, be active. I'm a simple man, and stick to the basics. It's done me well thus far.

Learn how to listen and how to work with your body. Pay attention to how you're feeling, don't ignore your body. Don't ignore your pain! The body is always communicating with you, and it's only right to listen. Imagine if you were trying to talk to someone you loved and they just kept ignoring you? You may start to harvest some anger or resentment, am I right? I know I would. Mostly though, I'd be sad. Our body is our friend. Our body is our vessel and our greatest tool. It's our vehicle to enjoy life! It's what allows us to witness and enjoy Earth's treasures. It allows us to embrace our loved ones. It allows us to explore. It allows us to feel. It allows us to create. Our bodies, they are the true Magic Wands."

Yang looks at his strong, calloused hands, then he rests them on the wooden railing. *"It's also important to check in with my family now and then. There are times when I can become consumed with a project and Yin or my little one will need to come to my rescue. Sometimes they know when it's time to rest, have a cup of tea, or play a game of make-believe even if I don't."*

Yang laughs, shakes his head, and sighs, acknowledging again the gratitude he has for his family. *"I say this to you because it's easy to forget sometimes. Focus, resilience, strength, and passion are all key components, but balance is where your true power lies. When your life is balanced, your power and inner strength are unwavering. You can only give to others as much as you have to give. As my beloved Yin always says, "You can't pour from an empty cup."*

His expression becomes serious, as he turns to face you. *"Never underestimate the power and wisdom of the feminine. The feminine spirit is to be honored and respected. Without Yin, I would most likely burn myself out. Without Yin, there would be no life. Yin has given birth to a spark of the Divine, for which I live and die. We are one unit, and as one we create a life of love, peace, and harmony; and when you have THAT in your heart, you are free. Nothing is more liberating. With peace in your heart, you have peace in your mind, and only then are you able to see what truly matters."*

Yang speaks with loving conviction. *"Before we go back inside, I need to tell you something. In case no one has ever said this to you, or if perhaps it's just been a long time since you've heard it, please know how much you are loved. You are loveable, and you deserve to ignite your soul with love. How we give and receive love is unique. You are safe to open your heart to love, and you are worthy of experiencing unconditional divine love. Begin with yourself, and the rest will follow.*

You are strong and courageous, more so than you have ever given yourself credit for. You have what it takes to bring forth into this world, whatever you believe in. You have the power to create the life you want, so long as you take inspired action toward your dreams, while at the same time, honoring your needs. Know your worth and realize your magnificence. You are safe to live authentically. You are safe to speak your truth, and you are worthy of being heard.

Be humble and kind. Sensitivity is not a weakness. We all live through our stories, we all have our truths, and it's okay to be different. Offer respect to others just the same as you would like it to be offered to you.

Be accountable for your actions and own your vulnerabilities. It's never too late to apologize, it's never too late to be forgiven, and it's never too late to change. Our egos are here to keep us safe, but sometimes they need to be courageously set aside, to let love in.

Question everything. Do not fear to look beyond what you are shown, and what you have known. Fear nothing when it comes to standing for what you believe in, yet be sure to question your beliefs and make sure they are rooted in love. Pierce through veils and illusions with courage. Bravely step outside your comfort zone. Step fully into your brilliant and powerful light, because the world needs you. You are protected, and forever will be. Please remember these words. Please don't ever forget."

Yang places his hand on your back and invites you into his arms for a long and loving embrace. He steps back as he opens the door and you both re-enter the house. You walk with Yang down the hallway, back to the family room where you join the beloved Yin and her child. You all take a seat upon the plush, earth-toned rug that is laid out across the hardwood floor.

You gaze out the west-facing, cathedral-shaped windows. The sunset has reached its peak through an exquisite display of color and light. A divine masterpiece has been painted and is witnessed by you in this very special moment, together with the family.

As you all sit, peering out the windows and watching the day end and the nighttime begin, you reflect upon what each of them has said to you throughout the day. They have given you so much to think about, so much to feel into, and so much to remember…

You extend your deepest and most sincere thanks before politely excusing yourself. You step outside into the front yard. Trillions of stars shine like brilliant diamonds, against the dark sky. It's quiet and very still. You walk toward a tree as it silently beckons you. You sit down and rest your back against the tree's solid trunk. You begin to recall times from your past, reviewing your life like a picture show being projected from your mind onto the backs of your eyes. Memories of stormy moments flood in, reminding you of all the disheartening times which left you feeling defeated. You cry for the heartbreaks, feeling the grief, sorrow, and anger as if they were happening all over again. You cry for the times of betrayal and abandonment, the times of loneliness and fear, and the times of crippling worry, uncertainty, and doubt. You realize these were all of the times you felt like giving up.

You've been through a lot and your heavy shoulders concur. You've experienced countless endings: relationships, friendships, jobs, homes. So many things throughout your life have faded away. Experiences you thought would last forever, are now gone. The pain you feel from reliving all of these moments is almost unbearable. It intensifies as you begin to see images of peoples' faces from your life.

You begin to see yourself through *their* eyes. You are taken down memory lane and shown how you've been on each side of the coin; the victim and the perpetrator. You are shown the times you were hurt, misunderstood, shamed, judged, abandoned, and betrayed, and the times when you have done the same to others. Conversations, arguments, and situations, are all now replayed to show you the impact you have had on others' hearts.

As you sit with the memories of these experiences, your body begins to remind you how it felt. Your heart begins to swell and ache; it hurts so bad. Your mind begins to torment you, sucking you into an emotional whirlpool of shame and regret. You see a chain of your past relationships, and as if they were linked together by mirrors, they begin reflecting and revealing the true meaning of compassion, and the importance of forgiveness.

You see the patterns you have been playing out, time and time again. These patterns have kept you stuck in a vicious cycle, and stem from a subconscious belief that you aren't worthy of experiencing anything different. Your subconscious rises to the surface and shows you all that has blocked you from experiencing your heart's true desires. You recognize how in so many instances, your *fear* of not being enough has been the only thing standing between you and your dreams.

The realizations are hitting you like lightning bolts, shaking you down to your core. You sob and grieve all over again from an entirely new angle, and at a deeper level, as it includes the hearts of so many others. Suddenly, a gust of wind rustles the leaves on the branches overhead and snaps you from your mind's paralyzing grip of remorse.

The Tree

"*Dear child, you're going to be alright. Don't be ashamed. Don't place judgment upon yourself. You are exactly where you need to be in perfect time, and you are perfect just as you are. There is no one, and nothing to blame, as everything that happens in life is part of the process.*

Forgive yourself for feeling as though things could have been different if only you knew then, that which you know now. Put down the heavy burden of guilt and shame. We only know that which we know, in the given time of where we are. You must be gentle with yourself as you grow and stretch to new heights of awareness. Your heart aches because you are gaining compassion and what a wonderful thing that is. Your heart is growing and expanding because you are feeling more, and learning how to love more.

Life unfolds and reveals to us what we need to know, all in perfect time. It's a process of infinite cycles through life and death. We learn, we grow, we change. People come, and people go. Everything and everyone evolves at their own pace. It's only natural; life continuously flows.

Everything and everyone is in their correct place, within their current cycle, as well as within the cycles happening all around them. Everything is moving, circling, and transitioning from birth to death, and back to life again. Within and without, as above so below, all of the cycles are beautifully interwoven and connected by a network of fine threads, quilted together as the fabric of time.

I know this may seem hard to grasp, My Child. The intricacies of consciousness are sometimes best left unknown. However, the more you wish to understand, you will most surely see, all in due time. It is through growth that you begin to see that which you are ready to know.

The unknown will open up to you, as you open yourself up to it. Open your eyes, open your mind, open your heart, and you will be blessed with ancient wisdom. Many secrets will be revealed to you, as long as you are not fearful of the dark. The deeper you dig, the closer you will come to the truth for all that you seek.

*Answers are typically hidden in plain sight although they are not always seen with the eyes. Have courage if you want to see new things, as they may be hard to face. So much exists around you, yet will never be fully known if you **only** look with your two eyes. Close your eyes and open your third eye, the eye that exists at the seat of the soul, where your heart and mind collide with all that is.*

Every single thing within your world of existence has something to show you, something to tell you, but to understand, you must attune your awareness. You must learn how to listen, and just as you can't see everything with two eyes, you can't hear everything with two ears. Use your body as an antenna. Allow yourself to feel all that which surrounds you, and listen for it to speak to you. Tune in your radio dial, ever so slowly, ever so precisely, until you hear the music.

Such a silly world we live in, isn't it? It's much like a puzzle and much like a game, but what fun it is! It's only a matter of shifting your perspective, Dear One. Slowly and surely, more and more of the picture is revealed, piece by piece. Life is not meant to be seen all at once.

You learn how to play, one level at a time. Patience and persistence are key. It is through trial and error that you find which pieces fit together. You learn how to play by trying new things, and if something doesn't work or doesn't fit, you try again! It can be frustrating, trying to find the piece you need to see more of the picture, but soon you will find it. Know that you will. The process of putting all the pieces together will create growth. This can be painful at times, yet it is nothing to fear and nothing to rush, and surely you must keep going.

I'm able to tell you these things because I've been around for quite some time, Dear One. I've cycled through many seasons and I've weathered many storms. My leaves are changing color and soon they will fall off, exposing my bare branches to the Winter's bitter cold winds and heavy *wet snow. Yet, it's only a matter of time until the buds on my branches burst forth and bloom again. Such is life; such is death.*

I wasn't always the wise and mighty oak you now sit beneath. Oh no! I started out as an acorn, just a tiny seed. I didn't understand the great potential held within me, to grow and expand into the mighty tree I am today. When I was a tiny seed, I fell from the tree that stands behind me now, do you see it?

I have experienced so much life! However, one night, a horrific storm with damaging winds came through, breaking off many of my branches. Only the strongest of them remained. I was already quite old at the time, and I just wasn't meant to hold onto everything as I once could. I surrendered to the strong winds and allowed the dead branches to break away.

When Yin and Yang saw what the storm had done to me, rather than chopping me down, Yang saw in me, the potential to become something new. He saw that what remained was very strong as my roots ran deep. Yang saw how I could become the perfect place to build a treehouse for his child. Yin agreed, so that's what he did. He transformed my trunk into a treehouse that would be of great joy to their little one, and this gave me a brand new purpose.

Indeed, I was a tiny seed that fell to Mother Earth, to Gaia. She took me into her soil and protected me. She gave me everything I needed to sprout up from inside the darkness of her earthly womb. She nurtured me and nourished me until I was ready to peek my head out into this welcoming world above. Even now she continues to nurture and nourish me in every moment.

I remember the first seasons of my life. The heavy rains and strong winds blew my young body around, yet I never broke. I was flexible and able to bend, which gave me resilience. You wouldn't have been able to lean against me though, back in my younger years, as I was still too young and not meant for that. I was still growing and becoming that which I did not yet know. I could only see as far as from my highest branch. Many years passed, and I continuously grew higher as my roots dug deeper into the soil.

In time, my trunk became thick and strong, and my foundation was solid, which allowed my branches to grow and reach up even higher. Eventually, they became strong enough to host families of birds, whether they stayed for a short rest, or chose to build a nest and stay longer, I was happy either way. I'm grateful for the birds that land on me. They keep me entertained with all their stories and adventures of flight. How grand it must be to be able to fly so free!

Dear Child, I feel you, as you rest against me. You hold too much; too many thoughts, too much stress, and too many worries and anxieties. Why? Tell me why you feel as you do. Release your worries, your fears, and doubts *unto me. Let me help you, share it all with me, allow yourself to cry, and let your tears run free. Your tears will purify your soul by allowing your emotions to flow. They will help you to release any impurities, any dense, stuck emotions that you have held within yourself. You will feel much better once you do.*

Please don't ever feel like you are alone, or like you don't matter. You are one of Mother Earth's creatures and you play a very special part just by being here. All of her creatures carry their unique gifts. All of her creatures have something special to offer.

Everything here on Earth exists together and all have a purpose. Whether what exists is something you like or dislike makes no difference, as it still has a purpose. It's up to you to discover what is for you and what is not.

May I remind you that you are much like me: a small seed, that has been birthed from a womb. Do you remember the potential that resides in your heart? Everything you need to grow into your version of a strong and mighty oak tree lies within you, and everything around you is here to help and support you. You can grow deep roots, establish a strong foundation, and reach great heights. You have your own medicine and perspectives to share. Your presence alone is needed more than you may ever know, and this alone provides your purpose. Share your stories, sing your songs, and express what you hold within. Release your unique creative genius out into the world. The divine intelligence of the ethers around you will receive all that you offer and will use it for the highest good of all.

There's so much more I can say to you, Sweet One, but that is enough for tonight. Come and sit with me anytime you would like to talk, rest, and reconnect with the ancient wisdom and unconditional love of Mother Earth. She is always here to hold and support you along your journey."

A gentle wind sends a single leaf cascading down from a branch above, floating and dancing its way onto your lap. You thank the tree for its gift and wrap your arms around its trunk, embracing it like your dear loved one.

As you walk away you can't help but notice the moon. It's full and bright, and its light illuminates the night sky, streaking out into the great expanse of stars. It offers you just enough light to safely navigate your way back to the house. Through the windows you see Yin and Yang sitting by the fireplace, and reading a storybook to their little one. A radiant loving glow emanates from the house.

You gaze up toward the sky once more and let out a sigh of relief in gratitude. Everything is finally beginning to make sense. The pieces are coming together, the bigger picture is forming, and it brings a smile to your face as you like what you see. With hope renewed, you open the door to go inside, knowing that you are exactly where you need to be; you are home.

It's time to rest, it's time to dream.
Life is not always as it may seem.

Storms will come and storms will go.
Lightning will strike and winds will blow.

Rain will fall to wash it away,
All being cleansed for a fresh new day.

Winter snow falls, Spring flowers sprout,
Autumn leaves change, Summer sun's out.

Things will die, yet new things will grow.
Do your best to remain in the flow.

Send your wishes up to the stars so bright.
Believe in them with all your might.

Honor your worth and trust your heart.
Know you can have a brand new start.

Let go of doubt and have no fear.
Help and guidance are always near.

What you seek you will surely find.
Listen to your soul, quiet your mind.

Love and light is what you are,
Shine forth like a radiant star.

Should you ever wonder what's real and what's true
Remember, the truth of who you are lives within you.

Workshopping with Spirit and Your Inner Family

The following pages of journal prompts will help you dive deeper and connect with the parts of yourself that need to be seen, heard, acknowledged, and explored. Feel free to use these pages in any way that speaks to your soul. Whether it be full sentences or just a few words, drawings, or quotes from the book that resonated, these prompts and pages are for you to express that which is on your mind and in your heart to be released through the magic of your hands. Approach these questions and reflections with openness and vulnerability. Be gentle and patient with yourself, allowing yourself time and permission to reflect. Tell yourself that you are safe as you delve into your shadows.

Call on Spirit to guide you, and help you see what you need to see. Call on Spirit to protect you, and to open you up to receive the healing that you are requesting, for your highest good, and the highest good of all involved.

Lastly, know that you're worth it and that the amount of energy you put into yourself will be reflected to you in miraculous ways.

What does the ideal child-like spirit feel like for you? What activities light you up and ignite that child-like sense of joy and excitement, where time seems to fly by?

If you could create your 'Dream Life,' what would that look like? Imagine all aspects of it, such as where you live, your job, your house, and your relationships.

What are you curious about? What sparks your interest? What would you like to learn more about? In what areas of your life could you embrace more of the child-like spirit?

When do you feel most safe?

If you had no fear, what would you do?

What prevents you from having more fun? When was the last time you allowed yourself to be silly?

When was the last time you allowed yourself to cry?

What makes you laugh? How could you introduce more laughter into your life?

When was the last time you allowed yourself to sing? To dance? To let your inner spirit be wild and free? To let loose without abandon, fear of judgment, or shame?

What are you passionate about? What's holding you back, standing in your way and preventing you from exploring your passions or from trying something new?

What helps you feel at peace? What brings you comfort? How do you nurture yourself?

What secrets do you hold within? How might you allow yourself to feel safe, to be more transparent, and to express any repressed emotions? Remember, you are forgiven and you are loved.

In what areas of your life do you feel shame and judgment, for yourself and others?

What are your non-negotiables, values and boundaries when it comes to your relationships?

Where have you felt like you have given your power away to outside sources?

What areas of your life feel imbalanced? Is there an equal energy exchange of give and take within the arenas of work, home, and social settings? Are the relationships in your life founded upon equal reciprocity? Does your life feel in harmony?

In what ways could you show yourself more love?

In what ways could you show others more love?

Can you look in the mirror and truly love what you see? Can you see and embrace your imperfections as true, unique beauty?

Explore the anger you hold within. Where do you feel it resides in your body?

Explore the sadness you hold within. Where do you feel it resides in your body?

Explore the resentment you hold within. Where do you feel it resides in your body?

Are there any experiences that you have not fully grieved? Bring your loving awareness to these moments and allow yourself to cry.

Where in your body do you feel pain? Can you bring your loving awareness to those parts and see what emotions arise? Listen and allow your body to speak to you.

Where can you offer more compassion for yourself and others in your life? Are you able to see yourself through another's eyes?

Where can you offer and practice more forgiveness? Can you allow yourself to forgive others? Can you allow yourself to forgive your past?

In what areas of your life can you let go of control? In what areas may you allow yourself to surrender to the Divine? In what situations may you allow yourself to trust more, and to flow?

Are there people/places/things that no longer bring joy to your life? Can you allow yourself to let them go with gratitude, ease and love? Give thanks to all you have learned and gained from them being a part of your life.

Can you allow yourself to let go of guilt? Remembering that you are worthy of saying, doing, and expressing what you truly want and feel?

In what areas of your life do you feel stuck or stagnant? Can you allow yourself to choose something new? Might you be able to try something different, or perhaps shift your perspective to see things through a lens of growth and opportunity?

Can you allow and give yourself permission to rest?

Can you allow yourself to say no? Can you be courageous enough to say yes? Practice speaking your authentic truth.

Can you permit yourself to unconditionally love yourself, forgive yourself, and know you are worthy of happiness, abundance, health, and peace?

Reflect upon any challenges within your life. Where are your opportunities for growth? What have they taught you? Are there any challenges that you can be grateful for? Have there been challenging relationships within your life that you can now be grateful for?

About the Author

D r. Melissa Crane has committed herself to a path of self-discovery and spiritual awakening. She willfully shares the wisdom she has gained and received, through her personal experiences and divinely channeled messages, with those who also seek to discover, remember, and awaken to the truth of who they are.

As a Holistic Chiropractor and Massage Therapist, Melissa has spent countless hours supporting and helping her clients heal through physical and emotional trauma.

Melissa now shares her wisdom and experience through teaching the sacred union of feminine, masculine and the child within; through traversing the dark night of the soul; by expounding the wisdom of Mother Earth; and by teaching you how to connect with Spirit.

Melissa serves as a Wayshower, a Teacher, a Healer, and a Guide to help you live a life of freedom and authenticity, and to assist you in co-creating your Heaven upon this New Earth.

Made in the USA
Monee, IL
10 August 2021

75412775R00069